WINE ALBUM

WINE ALBUM

Adapted from
MONSEIGNEUR LE VIN
Paris 1927

Text by Louis Forest
Illustrations by Charles Martin

The Metropolitan Museum of Art
Coward, McCann & Geoghegan.

THE *Wine Album* has been adapted from *Monseigneur le Vin,*
a book in the collection of The Metropolitan Museum of Art,
written by Louis Forest and illustrated by Charles Martin.
Monseigneur le Vin was first published in Paris in 1927
by Les Etablissements Nicolas.

A. Hyatt Mayor Purchase Fund, Bequest of Marjorie P. Starr,
1977 (1977.554)

Published in 1982 by The Metropolitan Museum of Art
and Coward, McCann & Geoghegan
All rights reserved.

LIBRARY OF CONGRESS CATALOGING IN PUBLICATION DATA

Wine album.

1. Wine and wine making.   I. Forest, Louis,
1872-1933. L'art de boire.   II. Martin, Charles,
1884-1934.

TP548.W75   1982   663'.2   82-8269
ISBN 0-87099-305-4
ISBN 0-698-11206-7 (Coward, McCann & Geoghegan)

PRODUCED BY
The Department of Special Publications,
The Metropolitan Museum of Art

Translated by Ormonde de Kay
Original design adapted by Peter Oldenburg
Printed and bound by A. Mondadori, Verona, Italy
Fourth Printing October 1983

Table of Contents

Preamble

Exordium

According to an old proverb, "When the wine is drawn one must drink it."

This is a deplorable maxim. It is certainly not the inspiration of a fine mind.

A gourmet would have written, "When the wine is drawn one must know *how* to drink it."

The civilized drinker

This title entails a code of conduct found only among superior beings. There is a potent difference between the ordinary drinker who gulps, swigs, and tosses off his glass and the man of taste who tenderly savors some masterpiece of vinous nature, exchanging appraisals and comparisons with wine lovers worthy of his confidence.

Le buveur civilisé

le Champion
du Sec
Regime

le
Gouliafre-

No excess

This little book is not addressed either to alcoholics or to un-discriminating boozers. It is for exquisites of the glass, for the rare and self-aware epicures whom I should like to see brought together. For myself, I am bound to say I am a sober gourmet; I hate excess in everything, it's sheer vulgarity. As Epicurus said, "Be moderate in order to taste the joys of life in abundance!"

So, neither a barfly nor a sot comes here to proclaim the pro-found beauty of a noble wine. When, slowly, blissfully, passionately, solemnly, amorously . . . respectfully, mystically, I raise to my lips a glass of wine to which the chosen soil, the life-giving sun, age-old experience, the loving care of experts, and the ripening of time have all contributed their best collaborative efforts; when my nose inhales and classifies the almost musical sensations—at that point, I warrant, the happiness that results is not merely corporeal, it awakens the very soul of my soul!

Education

Unfortunately, many people cannot savor secrets they regard as impenetrable or incomprehensible. Education is often to blame: the instructor has failed and no one has revealed the hidden beauties of wine. As a result, one may pass them by unaware, as one might walk unheeding across ground under which a treasure lies!

Often, too, the student of wine has not the gift of recognizing the refinement of the mouth, the nose, the tongue, and the taste buds. In such a case there is nothing to be done but to leave him to his fate and according to his temperament he will become either a drunkard or a prohibitionist—which amounts to the same thing.

La Cave

PART ONE
PREPARING

CHAPTER I

The wine cellar

I shall say nothing here about the loving attention vines require, or about the difficulties of the wine harvest, or about the care necessary for proper viniculture, or about the thousand and one ideas the winegrower must keep in mind if he wants the bottle you will serve at your table to be not just any glass container filled with vinegar, logwood residue, or bitter or oily acid, but an object of gustatory art, a supreme delectation, in short, a "bottle."

13

Let us move on to the wine cellar. Apart from the exceptions that prove the rule, does any Parisian still know what a wine cellar is? It is a dark room with thick walls, a cool and equable temperature, and an absence of vibrations.

Paris vibrates; its soil shudders; buses disturb the sleep of subterranean liquids. Central heating overheats; underground spaces are sewers through which pass electrical mains whose mysterious emanations exert influences, distantly, on wine that is as sensitive as an old coquette.

What became of the time when the wine cellar—the "library," as the Belgians still call it—was a place of veneration? There, bottles were arranged in rows and respected, like brooding hens. Their noble dust-covered immobility spoke to wine lovers of marvelous stories.

If you don't possess a wine cellar that is a wine cellar, but are nevertheless one of those very numerous creatures who have a vague idea that wine is better than mere drink, I dare to hope to make you initiates of the most spiritual of spiritual things, and I shall open to you the gates of the temple!

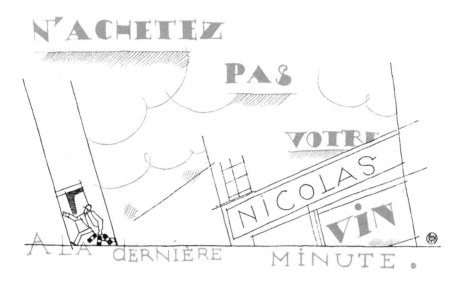

CHAPTER II

How to buy wine

To begin with, avoid the elementary mistake of buying wine at the last minute. Wine certainly isn't afraid of making trips—in the old days, to improve it, connoisseurs used to send it off on leisurely voyages to India and back—but when it is displaced it needs a rest, often a long one, before it is sacrificed to someone's pleasure. How many vintage wines have seemed poor because wine lovers, in too much of a hurry, uncorked them too soon after receiving them! I have known certain majestic bottles of Burgundy which, after a long displacement, have required more than a year of rest in order to regain their original beauty.

15

Thus, if you have friends to dinner, you musn't send out for wine just as you seat yourselves at the table, for while you have the right to drink badly, you never have the right to make others do so.

Let old bottles rest as long as possible, at least a week. They will repay you for your solicitude by awakening in beauty.

And here, a parenthetical comment. Let us dispose of the question of wine that is too old. It should be old, yes, but not senile. The antiquity of the label gives rise only to bitter regret when the liquid with the glorious name arrives only to expire, breathing its last in your glass! Wine should be an oldster who, retaining all of his lucidity, can happily attest to a long life and a gradual progression toward perfection. To present this charming conversationalist you mustn't wait until he is dead; a dinner is a generous interchange, not an interment. It is better to serve a wine that is too young than one that is too old.

Le vin doit être vieux

mais point sénile

From the bottle to the glass,
From the glass to the lips

The host, mindful of the consideration he owes the guests who have done him the honor of sitting at his table, should not be content just to buy bottles of the best provenance. Even if he knows they contain the fine flower of the most quintessential nectar from the happiest of centuries, his duty has only just begun.

They say there is many a slip 'twixt cup and lip, but the passage between bottle and cup is even trickier. I propose to serve as your guide on these two perilous voyages.

L'ÉLUE

CHAPTER III

How to prepare wine

Let us suppose you are going to serve an old red wine, a Burgundy that is full-bodied and sensual, like a man, or a Bordeaux that is supple and melodious, like a woman. I cite these two types of wine because one can't name them all, but the same truths apply to other vintages, whether those of the Côtes du Rhône, as vigorous as their Provençal sun, or the products of other plantings strong enough to age slowly over long periods without succumbing to senile decay. The "bottle" has been selected to match the menu and the guests. We now know which one will be the victim of the glorious sacrifice. But, the bottle still has to be transported from the wine cellar or storeroom to the place where it will be consumed. Careful! This is a delicate business.

Decanting

Old red wines have to be decanted. In the course of time they leave a deposit at the bottom of the bottle and the clear liquid has to be separated from this impure residue. To do this, one carefully decants the wine, making sure that no foreign matter is drawn into the stream. As a rule, one transfers wine in this way from the bottle to a decanter.

A friend of mine, an oculist, who had a keen nose for judging

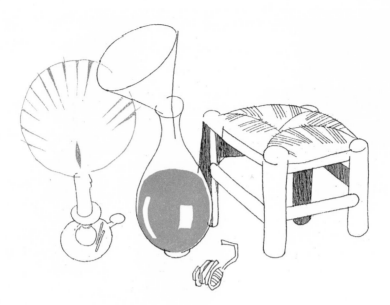

wine, once described the first part of the decanting process to me as follows: take your place before the rack of bottles with a lighted candle and, on the ground next to you, a little stool about a foot high.

A. Take the bottle from the rack, keeping it absolutely horizontal; if it comes from the front row, as soon as its neck is clear of the rack either lower it, still horizontal, or raise it—depending on whether you took it from a low or high part of the rack—to the level of the midpoint of your upper left leg. Then place your left foot on the stool so that your upper leg juts out at an angle of about 45 degrees. It goes without saying that if the bottle was originally in the rear row of the rack, the exact same procedure

Déboucher

must be preceded by your gently swinging the bottle around in the horizontal plane, thereby reversing it.

B. Bring the bottom of the bottle up and toward you until it rests atop your bent upper leg. With a levered corkscrew remove the cork smoothly, without any jerking motion. This done, advance the neck of the bottle to that of the decanter and effect the decanting, avoiding all knocks or bumps and checking the level of the sediment by the light of the candle, placed below the bottle.

By following the procedure outlined above, easier to perform than to describe, you obtain a decantation with a minimum of movement and hence a minimum likelihood of disturbing the wine.

Another method of decanting

To decant in a wine cellar, the first prerequisite is to have a wine cellar! But, as we said before, the wine cellar is dying, the wine cellar is dead! One might posit this mathematical and social law: the construction of wine cellars is in inverse ratio to that of bathrooms.

As we must never let hydrotherapeutics (again water, the enemy of wine!) deprive us of the great and glorious bottle, here is a method of decanting within the reach of apartment-dwelling gourmets.

Sentir le bouchon

A. Raise the bottle upright three or four days before the moment fixed for uncorking it and leave it immobile. This way, the lees gradually sink to the bottom.

B. Uncork with the greatest care at the appointed time, moving the delicate flask as little as possible, and smell the cork.

C. Just before decanting, light a candle and by its illumination examine the bottom of the bottle to determine where the deposit of lees is thickest.

D. Prepare, as indicated in the next section, the decanter that will be served at the table and insert in its mouth a glass funnel. To the right of the decanter place the lighted candle. Grasp the bottle in your right hand almost at the level of the bottom, making sure that the point where the deposit of lees is thickest (see Step C) is on the underside. Tilt the bottle slightly, using your left index finger as a fulcrum under its neck, then incline the bottle a little more to rest its paper or metal neckband gently on the rim of the glass funnel. Open your eyes—the decanting begins!

E. Pour slowly, slowly, slowly, slowly; the air should go back into the bottle in little bubbles, and any gurgling betrays unfortunate precipitancy. When the surface of the wine stretches out horizontally at its greatest length, speed up the pouring a little; at this moment the glow of the candle below should illuminate

Verser lentement

the bottle half-way up if it contains Burgundy or two-thirds of the way if one is decanting Bordeaux. Follow the progress of the little particles of sediment that advance perfidiously toward the exit, then slow down the operation so that the particles stay in the bottle and are not swept on by the last drops. The instant any of these residual bits present themselves in the neck, turn the bottle upright; not an atom of sediment can be allowed to spoil the visual purity of the wine in the decanter. This operation takes a long time to explain but is simple to accomplish. When it is properly carried out the amount of wine lost is insignificant—it should fit in a liqueur glass.

F. Stop the decanter with cotton wool. This stopper keeps dust from falling into the liquid. It shouldn't be too tight; air should circulate and oxidize the decanted wine, for the greater glory of man!

Capturing the bouquet

Preparing the decanter for decanting

There is, in every great bottle, a marvelous mystery that wine lovers have named the *bouquet*. This little genie, the fragrance of the wine, is extraordinarily sensitive. It is afraid of humidity, cold, and heat and will shrivel up and hide for the slightest reason. This timorous creature must be treated with infinite caution.

When, in a restaurant, you order a vintage wine of quality, the wine waiter often brings a flask delicately bedded down in a basket. But when the wine is cold, will the basket make it warmer?

Sometimes you are told that the bottle has been *chambré*, brought to room temperature. But what does that mean? More often than not the bottle has been set by the fire. The wine arrives luke-warm—awful! Heating is not bringing to room temperature.

If you wish the little genie to appear in its full glory, you must coax it in the manner we shall now describe. Just before the meal, fill a decanter with water as hot as the crystal can take without breaking; after a few minutes throw out the water. Then, take the bottle and pour half of a liqueur glass of wine into the scalded-out decanter, swirling it around and thus impregnating the entire inner surface with the fragrance. Then, slowly decant the rest of the bottle.

28

If you follow these directions, the wine's bouquet—the little genie—is aware of a temperate and sweet-smelling atmosphere, quits its deep hiding place, strolls about, and declares itself satisfied. All that remains is to sing its praises!

This problem of the bouquet is so important that I venture to cite here the advice of a Burgundian wine lover of exalted experience, Monsieur Charles Brunot. "This bouquet," he writes "is composed of some unstable ethers. Divine, born of celestial alcoholic spirits, they need oxygen to form and, to evaporate, a slight increase of heat. The object of decanting is not only to leave the lees or sediment at the bottom of the bottle, it also allows the molecules of ether to become oxidized on contact with the oxygen of the air. The only other alternative is to retain each mouthful a long time before swallowing, or to warm the wine industriously with your hands, but evaporation would then occur too late. One must consequently set this evaporation in motion by a preliminary, discreet raising of the temperature."

Such are the general rules.

And here, now, are some particular instructions.

Young and full-bodied red wines should be uncorked further in advance of drinking than less robust wines or those that have lost color. On occasion one can let them take the air for a whole day before their hour of giving pleasure.

The red Graves gain by being uncorked twelve or sometimes twenty-four hours in advance. On the other hand Margaux, Ludon, and so on lose by too prolonged an oxidation (except, however, in years when they are very full-bodied). Pauillacs,

Saint-Juliens, and Saint-Estèphes accommodate themselves in general to six or eight hours of breathing. Saint-Emilions and Pomerols need more time.

These tips are not, of course, at all definitive; the well-informed wine lover must determine the time of oxidation needed by the little genie of a given bottle in order for the wine to achieve the full measure of its blooming.

As a general rule, red Burgundies are not uncorked until the last minute; one avoids aeration, that is, oxidation. There are, however, exceptions. Sometimes, following a caprice of the thermometer or even of the barometer, wine seems too cool. The remedy is simple: the drinker, as noted, warms the glass in his fingers. Certain experts love to "incubate" their pleasure in this way; they are generally lovers of the vine, people who close their eyes when they drink in order to "hear" the wine!

White wines are not decanted.

Temperature

Red Bordeaux has to be *chambré,* that is, gently brought to a temperature at least as warm as that of the place where it will be drunk.

Red Burgundy is drunk at a temperature a little lower than that of the room.

As for white Bordeaux, the more elevated its birth, the more important it is that it be drunk cold. Cooling is not enough; it must

be iced. For this last operation, uncork the bottle before placing it in the ice bucket; replace the cork at your pleasure. Avoid aeration—that is, oxidation.

White Burgundy is served cool, but not iced. Uncork at the last minute. Avoid oxidation.

Champagne is served iced; this is not a new fashion. Documentation, dated June, 1667 reads: "We have conserved the ice of winter to moderate the ardors of summer. Our wines will be cool and delicious."

To ice wines, bring them out twenty minutes before consuming them; place them in an appropriately packed ice bucket; uncork, then replace the cork loosely. The wine should be neither too cold nor not cold enough!

Other wines—those of Anjou, Touraine, Alsace, the Rhine, etc.—benefit from being drunk very cool.

White port is served slightly cooler than room temperature, red port, a little warmer. If the latter contains sediment, it can be decanted. Port is indifferent to oxidation, but it is very sensitive to cold.

Madeira is served five or six degrees Celsius above room temperature.

Sherry, if it is mellow, should be served five degrees Celsius above the temperature of the place where it is consumed. If it is dry, five degrees Celsius below.

Wines made from liqueurs—Muscat, Banyuls, Malaga, etc.—are drunk at room temperature.

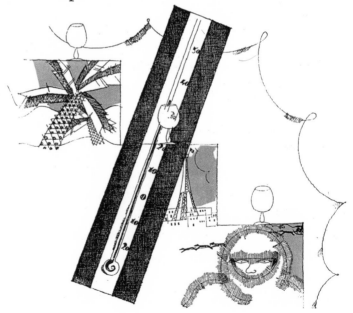

évitez
le
Verre
sans pied

PART TWO

SERVING

CHAPTER IV

How to serve wine
Crystal and glass

A wine connoisseur can be recognized at once by the glass out of which he drinks. To be sure, the cowl doesn't make the monk, but a monk would be unrecognizable without his cowl. And what heresies of latter-day crystal making have not been committed through failure to recognize and appreciate wine! You would think the people who make glasses never drink!

To start with, let's establish the fact that a glass without a stem cannot possibly go with a first-class wine. Its clumsy form is at home only in rough hands which, once the coarse drink in it is swallowed, will slam the glass on the table. It has a place on ocean

33

liners and in railway dining cars as a necessity, but how could it claim the honor of transmitting a noble product to worthy lips? A glass should allow people to admire the wine; that is its primary function. With the stemless glass, fingers hide the luminosities.

Certainly, during the Great War, we were less finicky. We drank from the bottle, out of mugs, out of whatever we could find. The spirit of wine arose, in spite of everything, out of rusty iron cups and chipped bowls. It was wartime! Today, we are trying to make civilization live again. That frail flower demands our sensitivity to nuance, choice, perfection.

The same reason that rules out the stemless glass—that the hand holding it extinguishes the luminous vibrations within it— likewise rules out the colored glass. Nature, with infinite delicacy, distills exciting hues, and who are we to destroy this marvel? The wine's lovely robe is a delight to contemplate, so why should we suppress, with opacities and colorings, this first harmony of the

Le
Verre
de
Coule

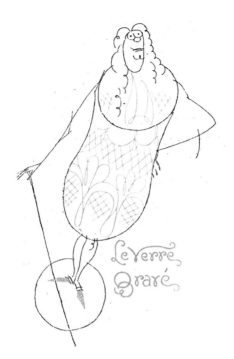

tasting ritual? Smash all glasses that are not transparent. Wine tasting, like love, begins with the eyes.

The fine wineglass is as radiant as possible, as pure as can be imagined, as thin as a human hair. It should make us pardon its presence by enabling us to forget that it is there. The slightest ornamentation mars it; a single stroke of an engraver can ruin its harmonious simplicity. All the more reason to avoid the sides, the masses, the flanges of crystal that break up beautiful geometric curves. Wine needs no other ornament than wine; it bears all its graces in itself.

If a glass should not block the viewing of wine, it most certainly should not interrupt the pleasure of the next source of enjoyment, the sense of smell. People of refinement insist that the actual absorption of wine has less importance, in terms of art, than the tasting of it by the olfactory system. To the stylish drinker, the nose is the dispenser of sensations; it distributes appetite to the nerve cells that moments later will open out in sensory fulfillment in the folds of the tongue and the palate.

These principles stated, the most perfect glass is undoubtedly the one whose crystalline paunch most nearly approaches a sphere. There are, indeed, balloon glasses of exquisite delicacy. Often, and it is an eminently commendable practice, the transparent belly tapers toward the top, so as to direct all the fragrance of the wine toward the nostrils. In this way a broad surface of evaporation is obtained and nothing is lost of the effluvia that, for the discriminating nose, make life more beautiful.

To my way of thinking the hierarchy of glasses, as established by usage reinforced by economy, is quite illogical. At a formal dinner one generally sits down before a complete assortment of glasses, the largest of which is the water glass. Why does water enjoy this privilege? I have never understood, either, why, at dinner parties, the Bordeaux glass, smaller than the water glass, should be bigger than the Burgundy glass. Pure routine, or, to be precise, impure routine! It corresponds to nothing logical, or even to what is simply appropriate.

Our vintage wines, whichever they may be, are endowed with divers aromas and pleasing shades of color. To serve this pleasure while diminishing it by putting it in too small a glass is, in truth, a bad joke. And since the total, superior sensation afforded by

pourqupi?

first-class wine is made up of a combination of joys of the eye, the tongue, the palate, and the intelligence, obstructing the yield of fragrances by too small a glass amounts to destroying one of the essential elements of sensual delight.

The preceding laws being established, there emerges an inescapable corollary: never fill a glass more than half full. Stay, indeed, below that level, even well below it. Then the little genie that was in the bottle will take its ease and disport itself freely for the satisfaction of your nose and the very charm of life.

The long and short of it is that a stemmed glass should be of ample size, thin, light, well-balanced, and firmly based, bearing no engraving, no graining or veining, and no facets. The cup and the sphere should not widen out at the mouth but on the contrary tend to narrow, like a tulip. The stem, like the leg of an elegant woman quite uninterested in vain adornments on her stockings, is not embellished with rings or decorations that break up its smooth line; neither square nor hexagonal nor octagonal, it remains soberly cylindrical. The height of the glass's lower part, base and stem together, should be slightly less than that of the actual receptable—two-thirds or three-quarters, but never more. The base can only be round.

Such is the "canon" of a tasteful wineglass.

We might add that certain gourmets have adopted the practice of serving great wines in even greater glasses. In these enormous vessels liqueur brandy, when of high quality, expands powerfully. For wines, however, their use is subject to criticism. The whites oxidize in them and lose their coolness too quickly, while somewhat delicate reds do not sufficiently concentrate their fragrance therein, beneath the probing nose.

And now, a general rule: when an artist imagines a model glass, he should remember that it is not His Highness the Wine who must adapt himself to the glass but the glass that must submit to the requirements of His Highness the Wine!

Monseigneur le Vin

Adapting the wine to the menu

Hostesses are often in a quandary when planning to serve several wines with several different dishes.

Which should they serve first?

Just as there are colors that go together—just as green usually likes the contrast of black but dreads being juxtaposed with maroon—certain tastes either pair off happily or reject one another. No one can be unaware that a fine Saint-Emilion—or, better yet, a vintage Burgundy—enhances the taste of prime Roquefort. The reverse is likewise true.

It is this physical law that enables us to solve a problem gourmets have been discussing since time immemorial, like baccarat players eternally arguing whether or not to draw a fifth card, to wit: should one serve a sweet before the cheese, or should the cheese come first? In theory and in general the order is *salt, sugar.* Salt food precedes sweet. Cheese, then, if the rule is law, should be served before a sweet dish. Such was the opinion of Talleyrand, a great gourmet of cheese (which was, as it happens, the one regime to which he remained faithful all his life).

But in practice, a case could be made for the opposite order. It all depends on your guests. If they are wine lovers, don't hesitate to serve cheese at the end of the meal, for to a connoisseur the flavor of a vintage red wine blending with the taste of a paste of fermented milk ripe for the eating is the very key to paradise. The dessert, in this case, is the wine.

But if your guests are not initiates, don't hesitate a minute. Take away the red wines, serve the dessert after the cheese and accompany it with a sweet white wine or a dessert wine.

Another problem: should one vary the wines at a big dinner? Paul says yes, Peter says no. I believe it is preferable to say yes. Except in the case of champagne, the sensation a wine imparts tends to become blunted rather quickly, so variety, as well as choice, is called for. I hasten to add, however, that when the foods complement the wine, certain vintages hold their own splendidly throughout a meal.

Some general rules

A. Do not serve a full-bodied wine before a lighter or less *enveloppé* wine, for example a red Burgundy before a red Bordeaux, or port before either.

B. Do not serve sweet wine before dry, for example a Sauternes or an Anjou before a Chablis.

Faites enlever les verres

LE VIN
LE PLUS
FORT
CHASSE
LE PLUS DELICAT

C. Avoid serving red wine after a liqueur-like white wine, for example a red Bordeaux after a Sauternes or a Château-Margaux after a Château-Yquem.

D. Throw out guests who mix their wines and never invite them again.

If, by bad luck, you have to humor these savages, remove their wineglasses, even if they are still full, as each new course is served. It's a shame that false propriety doesn't permit this procedure. When gourmets come to reign over society it will become good manners to do so.

These rules don't need to be explained. A strong wine drives out a more delicate one. Since the white wines of Sauternes and

Anjou are sweeter and mellower than the vintage reds, the latter seem skimpy when they follow the former. It is, in sum, simple.

And yet how many consumers are there, how many men in the wine trade even, who are unaware of this elementary rule, and who are sufficiently boorish to recommend that a person serve Madeira, sherry, or port before the meal or with the soup! It brings tears to my eyes! To impose a reagent of this sort on the palate at the beginning of dinner is to brutalize it for the remainder of the meal. The taste buds will have a hard time "recovering," as boxers say, from this knockout punch.

Enhancing the flavors

Wines and dishes ought to enhance each other. It would be foolish to treat the matter as a battle of tastes when earthly happiness comes from concord. Thus, as the slightest experience shows, red Bordeaux wines clash with vinegary or overly sweet food. But how well an old red wine sets off crayfish! Lyric prose writer Maurice des Ombiaux declares that while pastries and fruits don't go at all with red Burgundy, the sensation is nevertheless magnificent when, in summer, the rare wine of the Côte-d'Or accompanies a slice of ripe melon, well iced!

A few snippets of information will throw light on these questions, vast as the world, varied as humanity, so sweet to experience!

Le poisson appelle le vin blanc

Fish calls for white wine except when it is prepared in a stew, in which case it calls for red. Chablis and Pouilly almost seem to have been dreamed up by the gods to accompany oysters and cold fish.

A Haut–Barsac or a dry white Burgundy harmonize to perfection with fish.

A Montrachet deifies a galantine, ham, or cold poultry.

Some people maintain (though I myself am not altogether of their opinion) that port can go with lobster *à l'armoricaine*—or, as other people call it, *à l'américaine*—with crayfish, and with fish pies seasoned with both pepper and spices.

A reliable Madeira or a dessert wine accompanies fruits or dessert.

As a rule, the serving of red wine does not continue up to the serving of the sweet, except, as noted previously, in the case of cheese fanciers who are fatally fond of Burgundy and Saint-Emilion or have a weakness for an Hermitage or a Châteauneuf-du-Pape.

As noted earlier, sweet dishes go with sweet white Bordeaux wines, with certain Anjous, some of which are remarkably pleasant, and with certain wines of Touraine, including some that are quite exceptional.

What else do I know?

As to champagne, if it is a dry type, and if it accompanies the entire meal, it should not continue to be served after the cheese and after dessert. Even so, at grand banquets in which the cup (Oh! how I miss the old flute glass that let stars fly up in the wine!) sustains toasts and speeches and orations, champagne regularly terminates the proceedings. In these circumstances, as it accompanies fruits and candies, it should preferably be light and slightly sweet.

In sum, the practice of serving champagne at the end of a meal seems heretical. This wine—let's say it in a good, loud voice—should precede all other wines, and it is at the very beginning of the meal that it should be served, dry or semi-dry, of course. If champagne only is to be served throughout the dinner, one can vary and harmonize the sensations, proceeding from dry to semi-dry and ending up with the very sweetest, just before dessert.

Let me hasten to proclaim that the laws I have just promulgated do not constitute a narrow and punitive body of legislation; they should be obeyed in spirit rather than to the letter. A host who respects his guests enough to study the dishes he has selected and present them in a skillful progression has the right, knowing his wines and his wine cellar, to vary gustatory pleasures according to affinities known to him alone. The service of wines should be a symphony!

There remains a controversial question: what should one serve with *hors d'œuvre variés,* condiments in oil, Turkish-style eggplant, artichoke hearts, vegetable salad with mayonnaise, and the like?

In the presence of hors d'œuvres which taste acid or very pronounced, the best of wines gives up. It confesses itself annihilated, flattened. Graver still, all its charm seems deflated; it is, if I may be excused the bold comparison, like a fine top hat stoven in by the blow of a fist.

Certain suggestions are dropped in your ear: "With this kind of hors d'œuvre, serve an aggressive little rosé from the Aube or Lorraine." So be it, if you like, but perhaps there's a better way.

*Le service
des vins doit être une symphonie*

Two solutions present themselves. I shall whisper them in your ear, very low, for I would make too many enemies if I revealed them out loud.

Here is the first. When wondering what wine to serve in these circumstances, there is one sure-fire means to extricate yourself from your quandary: don't serve hors d'œuvres! I myself don't appreciate them much. Most often they owe their essential flavor to vinegar (*vinaigre*), which isn't or shouldn't be anything but sour wine (*vin aigre*).

Il a mal tourné

A second solution: if you absolutely insist on those hors d'œuvres and are looking for the beverage that best matches their gustatory aesthetic, then, instead of wine, pour water—yes, water, cool, clear, light. To wash down hors d'œuvres water is surely the most suitable drink—water which, washing the palate clean, prepares it to receive the more classic sensations that will soon follow.

Let me be clearly understood. My disdain for hors d'œuvres does not extend to despising *amusettes variées,* the kinds of pre-meal pastries, generally hot, to which great culinary artists sometimes give unexpected, attractive, and witty forms. No, I only protest against those acid and gelatinous hors d'œuvres which are too often put to the dubious purpose of accommodating leftovers.

Following the same line of thinking as before, what wine can go with salad? I haven't any idea. It is preferable, then, not to drink at all during this formality, which fulfills a certain hygienic function but which numerous gourmets banish from their tables since it can only needlessly prejudice the serving of wines.

Foods that do and do not go with red wines

Recommended Foods

Ham and cheese pie
Brochettes of kidneys with bacon
Lamb
Mutton
Beef
Veal
Fowl
Game
Starchy vegetables
Mushrooms
Game pie
Goose liver pâté
Cheeses: Cheshire, Gruyere, Roquefort, Dutch cheese, Emmenthaler, Camembert

Proscribed Foods

Hors d'œuvres in oil and vinegar dressing
Shellfish
Eggs
Pasta
White sauce and Madeira sauce
Green vegetables
Salads with oil and vinegar dressing
Cream cheese
Any and all sweet and sweetened dishes

Certain dishes call for light, fragrant wines and certain others for full-bodied wines with a very pronounced taste.

Foods that do and do not go with white wines

Recommended Foods

Oysters
Hot and cold fish
Crayfish *armoricaine*
Timbales and vol-au-vents of chicken
Sweetbreads
Roast fowl
Chicken with rice
Lamb
Ham
Goose liver in aspic
Galantines
Sweets and glazed biscuits
Skim-milk cheese
Dried almonds

Proscribed Foods

Hors d'œuvres in oil and vinegar dressing
Roast beef
Madeira sauce
Creamed vegetables
Salads and other dishes in oil and vinegar dressing
Cream cheese

With oysters and fish, very aromatic dry and semi-dry wines are preferable; with meat, liqueur-like wines, and with dessert, very liqueur-like wines, i.e., wines that are still, sweet, and soft.

Wines that go with various foods

White Wines

A. Foods with which DRY white wines are preferable:

Oysters, shellfish

Eggs

Lobster or crayfish mayonnaise
Cold fish mayonnaise
Grilled fish
Fried fish

Roast fowl

Duck with olives
Duck with turnips

Roast lamb

Braised lettuce
Celery *au jus*
Endives *au jus*
Turnips *au jus*
Cauliflower with cheese sauce

Freshwater crayfish

Galantines
Ham

Glazed biscuits

B. Foods with which MELLOW or semi-dry wines are preferable:

Bouchées à la reine
    (vol-au-vent of chicken)
Sweetbreads
Timbales
Tripe *à la mode de Caen*
Vol-au-vent

Bouillabaisse
Lobster *armoricaine*
Sole *normande*
Fish in melted butter
Oily or semi-oily fish

Sautéed chicken
Chicken marengo
Chicken chasseur

Chicken with rice

Asparagus with melted butter

Cardoon (edible thistle)
New kidney beans
Artichoke hearts
String beans
Lentils

Spaghetti, noodles, macaroni
Baby green peas
Potatoes

Goose liver

Desserts and sweets

52

Red Wines

A. Foods with which LIGHT wines are preferable:

Ham and cheese pie
Brochettes of kidneys with bacon
Lamb cutlets
Leg of lamb
Saddle of lamb
Lamb Villeroy
Roast veal
Sweetbreads
Grilled mutton chops
Giblets
Roast lark
Roast quail
Roast young turkey
Roast thrush
Roast partridge

Roast pigeon
Roast Guinea fowl
Roast chicken
Chicken stew (*poulet en cocotte*)

New kidney beans
Braised lettuce
Lentils
Baby green peas
Potatoes *maître d'hotel*
New potatoes with butter

Goose liver
Pâtés of the game above

B. Foods with which wines that are FULL-BODIED or endowed with a strong aromatic savor are called for:

Leg of mutton with string beans
Stewed mutton
Saddle of mutton with vegetables

Beef $\begin{cases} \text{beefsteak} \\ \text{filet mignon Perigueux} \\ \text{tenderloin, sirloin} \\ \text{rumpsteak} \\ \text{grilled tournedos} \\ \text{tournedos Rossini} \end{cases}$

Duck $\begin{cases} \text{roast duck} \\ \text{Rouen-style duck} \\ \text{with olives} \\ \text{with turnips} \end{cases}$
Cassoulet of goose
Duck's liver Perigueux
Boned and broiled pigeon
Chicken $\begin{cases} \text{chasseur} \\ \text{marengo} \end{cases}$

Woodcock

Snipe

Venison

Pheasant
Hare
Partridge with cabbage
Wild boar
Teal

Cardoon (edible thistle) *au jus*
Celery *au jus* or braised
Bordeaux mushrooms
Cauliflower with cheese sauce
Artichoke hearts
String beans with bacon
Potatoes with bacon

Pâtés of the game above

PART THREE

DRINKING

CHAPTER V

How to drink wine

Bearing

Here is an important chapter that will reveal to you the essential difference between the act of swallowing and the art of drinking.

Mental Preparation

The wine lover is recognizable by his bearing: he has very distinctive deportment. Monsieur Mathieu, the celebrated professor of enology, has described him with extraordinary precision. I borrow a few words from him here (for one only borrows from the well-to-do) and I summarize.

The drinker gets ready to drink. He concentrates all his faculties of attention on his glass.

Préparation mentale

Pleasure of the eyes

The glass is filled halfway up. The drinker tilts it so as to enjoy the colors, varying the strata of liquid. He admires the hues, which range from white, gilt, and pink to ruby red and purplish brown, even to that straw-colored yellow to which the play of light sometimes adds a ray of emerald.

Plaisir des yeux

Pleasures of the nose and brain

The surface of the wine being kept horizontal, one inhales gently to smell the bouquet. One intensifies the olfactory impression by moving the glass so as to cause the liquid to rotate. This dance encourages the effluence of volatile ingredients through agitation and exposure to the air.

To effect this gyratory movement, the law and the prophets recommend taking the body of the glass delicately between thumb and forefinger, the other three fingers remaining free and half bent, fanwise, and commencing the rotation from right to left, that is, counterclockwise. This agitation transforms the horizontal surface of the wine into a parabolic surface and enrobes with wine the free upper part of the glass's inner side. Then the olfactory sense is dilated by the gamut of scents, some subtle and others penetrating. Then, too, the wine lover strives to individualize and characterize these fragrances, and to compare them with bouquets gathered in and analyzed on previous occasions. It is a delicious moment.

Plaisir du nez

Pleasures of the mouth, tongue, and palate

At this point one drinks delicately, in sips, like a bird. One lets each mouthful flow back into the mouth, the better to analyze it. It is important to know that "the shores of the tongue have special sensibilities." The exceptional taster does not fail at this moment to purse his lips; he sucks in a little air to make the wine bubble at the temperature of the mouth. At that instant a new series of scents and tastes rise from the glass to the upper regions of the intellect. Then begins the majestic, religious, ideal, and definitive moment of . . .

Plaisir de la bouche

Appreciation

The head bends forward, expression grows serious and the drinker, gathering up memories from the depths of his soul and garnering, by means of his intellect, old and long-buried sensations, sets up as a judge. Then he and his companions discuss and compare. They know the great years without going all the way back to the celebrated one of Halley's Comet (1811).

L'appréciation

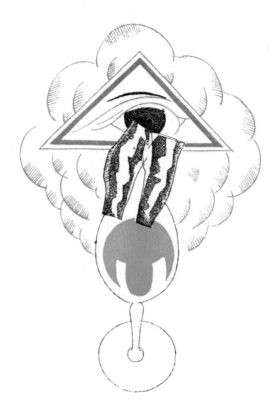

Now the wine lovers exchange opinions which, for the profane, remain mysterious. The ignorant or uncivilized individual doesn't realize that a wine "with its hat on its ear" is a liquid pierced by a tip of acidity and beginning to turn sour, or that a wine having "a waistcoat" is an opulent wine, well constituted and masculine, the wine, in short, of a serious and healthy gentleman, while wine that has "a bosom" is more delicate and more feminine—well made, too, but finer and more amorous.

In general, gourmets of the first rank are content to distinguish a wine's "body," its "robe," its "sweetness" or "dryness," its "*sève*" (aromatic savor), its "bouquet," and its "fragrance." Top-ranking wine lovers naturally employ a much richer language, and their imaginations dictate new vocabularies with each drop consumed.

For "robe" alone there are at least a hundred different expressions, each prettier and more striking than the last. They describe hues as various as nature itself and measure innumerable gradations of transparency: from white to yellow to red to brown, from clear amber to oxblood ruby, and from old gold to that onionskin pink that charms the viewer in certain bottles from Alsace or the Côtes du Rhône.

These magical movements of hand, nose, lips, and tongue, these exchanged comments, these comparisons, judgments, memories— all together, they inspire confidence in life. At this instant a man can say, "I am happy."

RÈGLE DE NOBLESSE

Vocabulary

It is advisable, in classifying a wine, to consider its

1. General constitution: body, finesse, equilibrium

2. Vinosity

3. Color or robe

4. Smoothness or harshness, resulting from the percentage of sugar, acid, tartar, tannin, etc., in it

5. Bouquet and taste, resulting from the essential ethers perceived by the senses of smell and taste, respectively

1. General Constitution

Vocabulary of Qualities	Vocabulary of Defects
Complete, well furnished	
Full-bodied	Thin
Fleshy, well fleshed	Puny
Muscular	
Well wrapped, stuffed	Skimpy
Full, nourished	Skinny, a breadboard
Solidly based	
Robust, vigorous	
Well balanced	Badly balanced
That has body	Badly turned out, badly built
That has flesh	Awkward, ungainly
Chewable	
Firmly based	
That has a foundation	
That has a frame	
Well built	
What a colossus!	
That has stomach	
That has a waistcoat	
That has a bosom	

QUIA DU CORSAGE

Fine, delicate	Coarse, common
Agreeable, elegant	
Serious, that has bearing	Frivolous, that has frills and furbelows

Vocabulary of Qualities	Vocabulary of Defects
That has the stamp of superiority	Plebeian
That has class	A lout
A lord!	

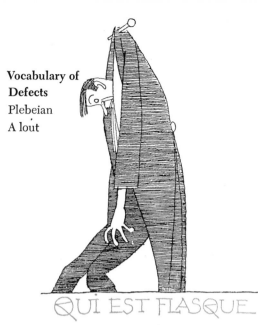

QUI EST FLASQUE

2. Vinosity

Nervous	Dull
Heady, exhilarating	Flat
Potent	Limp
	Feeble, lymphatic
Generous	Poor
That has warmth	
That has fire	Cold
Closely packed	Anemic, degenerating

3. Color or Robe

Brilliant	Cloudy
	Worn out
Scintillating	Lusterless
Alive with color	Overcast
Amber	
Ruby	That has too much robe

71

Vocabulary of Qualities	Vocabulary of Defects
Reddish brown, tawny gold	
Stripped bare	Overdressed
Onionskin (purplish brown)	
Pretty	That has an ugly robe
That has "eye" (luster, sheen)	Badly dressed

4. Smoothness or Harshness

Mellow	Acid
	Rough
	Rough surfaced
	Acrid
Tender	Green
	Astringent
	Bitter
Supple	Harsh
	Uncivilized
	Arid
Firm	Raw
Round	Sharp pointed
Flowing	Dry
Melted	Watery
Velvety	Biting
Unctuous	Aggressive
Thick	That rasps
Flowing	That has roughnesses
Silky	That scratches
	Hot, burning

QUI A LE CHAPEAU
SUR L'OREILLE.

Vocabulary of Defects

That pricks, stings
Sour, tart
That has a point
That has back strain
That has its hat on its ear
Whose cap is falling off

5. Bouquet and Taste

Pure
Bouqueté, that has bouquet
That has nose
Fragrant
Truffled, raspberry flavored, etc.
Nutty taste, peach taste, etc.

That has sap
In the full rising of the sap

Well preserved, that holds up

Fruity
Full flavored

Sick, stale
Flat

Rancid
That smacks of the soil
Foxtail taste (as if made from the
    last of the grapes — the tailings)
Tired, worn
That assumes the properties of age
That takes a header
Passé
Emaciated, gaunt
Dead
Sullied
Extinguished

Vocabulary of Qualities	Vocabulary of Defects
Lively	Deflated
Wide awake	Doughy
Sharp, smart	Heavy
Gay, brisk	Thick, pulped
Appetizing, arousing	Dull, tame
Shameless, profligate (wow!)	Boring
That stretches out	That stops short
Attractive	Stupid
Exciting	Insignificant
Seductive	Lacking charm
Evocative	Unattractive
Engaging	
Amorous	Severe
Sensual	Austere, ill-tempered
Voluptuous	
That has "dog" (i.e., charm, fascination)	
Full of zest	
That spreads in a peacock tail	
That talks well	
That sings	Mute
Rich, that ends stylishly	Untidy, in disarray, that ends in flounces and furbelows

QUI A du CHIEN

CONCLUSION

Be careful to whom you offer it

And now, an essential piece of advice. It is sacrilege to offer a vintage wine to just anybody. It's like casting pearls before swine. One only serves first-class bottles to wine lovers knowledgeable enough to appreciate them, or, at a pinch, to young people endowed with the internal finesse that affords reason to hope they will one day be completely educated in matters of taste.

Pierre de Ronsard, the most gracious of our poets, was born long ago at Couture in the Touraine. His father, the Chevalier Loys de Ronsard, owned a charming manor house there, a home fit for a scholar and wit. He was sensual and pleasure loving, but always within limits, as became a cultured gentleman who knows that nothing lasts except through moderation and that if one doesn't want overindulgence to put an end to use, one must not ignore the pious precepts counseling the avoidance of excess. So his dwelling was full of both dignity and taste; everything was in its place, in that particularly felicitous manner in which well-read people with a knack of arranging things know how to ennoble their surroundings.

One could admire there, for example, a beautiful chapel for the veneration of God, a good kitchen for the cultivation of the body, and a double wine cellar for the simultaneous veneration of both.

Like the entire house, the wine cellar was decorated with inscriptions carved in stone. They have not disappeared. One can still decipher these mottoes of lapidary philosophy. One of them, for example, says, "Before Leaving."

These two words signified that the master of the house wanted to taste the good things of this world as much as possible before the hour of his death. This maxim, "Before Leaving," was carved over the entrance to the vault of fine wines. And that reminds me of a friend of mine who, feeling that he was about to give up the ghost, had an old bottle of Burgundy he had been saving for a great occasion sent up to him. He said to us, "I shall not leave it in my estate. Now see how a man drinks who is going off to digest in another world!" He, too, was bent on tasting his fine wine "before leaving."

AVANT
PARTIR

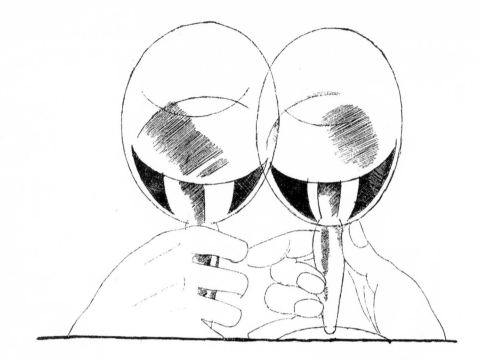

Loys de Roncard's wine cellar was divided in two. In one store-room was the *Vinum Barbarum*. This should not be translated as "barbarous wine," the phrase simply means ordinary wine, table wine.

The vault of rare wines was just next door. It was decorated with an inscription I ask you to think about, for it is what will make worthwhile to you these last few lines blending history, poetry, and wine. It read *Cui des Videto:*

"Be careful to whom you offer it."

And now, reader, that I have done my best to teach thee how to drink according to the grand traditions, let's clink our glasses and toast each other's health in the antique manner:

I: *A la tienne!*
Thou: *Sensible.*
I: *De tout coeur!*
Thou: *Mêmement.*

And the two of us in unison: *Comme de juste!*

Monseigneur le Vin

RECORD OF YOUR WINES

To remove a wine label, either soak the bottle in hot water or rotate it in the steam over a kettle of boiling water for fifteen minutes (more if the glue is particularly adherent). Another method is to wet four or five paper towels with warm water, wrap them around the bottle, and let the bottle stand for one and one-half hours. For more stubborn cases, careful scraping with a single-edged razor blade may be necessary.

Allow the label to dry before gluing it into the book.

Fresh labels can sometimes be obtained by writing to the vintner indicated on the label.

If you are not successful with the above, or if it is not appropriate to take the bottle home, simply write the label information in the space provided.

NAME OF WINE: _____

VINTAGE YEAR: _____

VINTNER: _____

REGION: _____

La cave

ATTACH YOUR WINE LABEL HERE

La Cave

PURCHASED AT: _____

PRICE: _____ DATE: _____

SHARED WITH: _____

_____ DATE: _____

PLACE: _____

MENU: _____

PERSONAL RATING: _____

COLOR: _____ BOUQUET: _____

TASTE: _____

NAME OF WINE: _____

VINTAGE YEAR: _____

VINTNER: _____

REGION: _____

L'ÉLUE

ATTACH YOUR WINE LABEL HERE

L'ÉLUE

PURCHASED AT: _____

PRICE: _____ DATE: _____

SHARED WITH: _____

_____ DATE: _____

PLACE: _____

MENU: _____

PERSONAL RATING: _____

COLOR: _____ BOUQUET: _____

TASTE: _____

NAME OF WINE: _____

VINTAGE YEAR: _____

VINTNER: _____

REGION: _____

Le vin doit être vieux

ATTACH YOUR WINE LABEL HERE

Le vin doit être vieux

PURCHASED AT: _____

PRICE: _____ DATE: _____

SHARED WITH: _____

_____ DATE: _____

PLACE: _____

MENU: _____

PERSONAL RATING: _____

COLOR: _____ BOUQUET: _____

TASTE: _____

NAME OF WINE: _____

VINTAGE YEAR: _____

VINTNER: _____

REGION: _____

ATTACH YOUR WINE LABEL HERE

PURCHASED AT: _____

PRICE: _____ DATE: _____

SHARED WITH: _____

_____ DATE: _____

PLACE: _____

MENU: _____

PERSONAL RATING: _____

COLOR: _____ BOUQUET: _____

TASTE: _____

NAME OF WINE: _____

VINTAGE YEAR: _____

VINTNER: _____

REGION: _____

ATTACH YOUR WINE LABEL HERE

PURCHASED AT: _____

PRICE: _____ DATE: _____

SHARED WITH: _____

_____ DATE: _____

PLACE: _____

MENU: _____

PERSONAL RATING: _____

COLOR: _____ BOUQUET: _____

TASTE: _____

NAME OF WINE: _____

VINTAGE YEAR: _____

VINTNER: _____

REGION: _____

ATTACH YOUR WINE LABEL HERE

Cueillez Le Bouquet

PURCHASED AT: _____

PRICE: _____ DATE: _____

SHARED WITH: _____

_____ DATE: _____

PLACE: _____

MENU: _____

PERSONAL RATING: _____

COLOR: _____ BOUQUET: _____

TASTE: _____

NAME OF WINE: _____

VINTAGE YEAR: _____

VINTNER: _____

REGION: _____

Qui A du CHIEN

ATTACH YOUR WINE LABEL HERE

QUI A du CHIEN

PURCHASED AT: _____

PRICE: _____ DATE: _____

SHARED WITH: _____

_____ DATE: _____

PLACE: _____

MENU: _____

PERSONAL RATING: _____

COLOR: _____ BOUQUET: _____

TASTE: _____

NAME OF WINE: _____

VINTAGE YEAR: _____

VINTNER: _____

REGION: _____

ATTACH YOUR WINE LABEL HERE

PURCHASED AT: _____

PRICE: _____ DATE: _____

SHARED WITH: _____

_____ DATE: _____

PLACE: _____

MENU: _____

PERSONAL RATING: _____

COLOR: _____ BOUQUET: _____

TASTE: _____

NAME OF WINE: _____

VINTAGE YEAR: _____

VINTNER: _____

REGION: _____

ATTACH YOUR WINE LABEL HERE

La temperature

PURCHASED AT: _____

PRICE: _____ DATE: _____

SHARED WITH: _____

_____ DATE: _____

PLACE: _____

MENU: _____

PERSONAL RATING: _____

COLOR: _____ BOUQUET: _____

TASTE: _____

NAME OF WINE: _____

VINTAGE YEAR: _____

VINTNER: _____

REGION: _____

ATTACH YOUR WINE LABEL HERE

POURQUOI !

PURCHASED AT: _____

PRICE: _____ DATE: _____

SHARED WITH: _____

_____ DATE: _____

PLACE: _____

MENU: _____

PERSONAL RATING: _____

COLOR: _____ BOUQUET: _____

TASTE: _____

NAME OF WINE: _____

VINTAGE YEAR: _____

VINTNER: _____

REGION: _____

Monseigneur le Vin

ATTACH YOUR WINE LABEL HERE

Monseigneur le Vin

PURCHASED AT: _____

PRICE: _____ DATE: _____

SHARED WITH: _____

_____ DATE: _____

PLACE: _____

MENU: _____

PERSONAL RATING: _____

COLOR: _____ BOUQUET: _____

TASTE: _____

NAME OF WINE: _____

VINTAGE YEAR: _____

VINTNER: _____

REGION: _____

ATTACH YOUR WINE LABEL HERE

PURCHASED AT: _____

PRICE: _____ DATE: _____

SHARED WITH: _____

_____ DATE: _____

PLACE: _____

MENU: _____

PERSONAL RATING: _____

COLOR: _____ BOUQUET: _____

TASTE: _____

NAME OF WINE: _____

VINTAGE YEAR: _____

VINTNER: _____

REGION: _____

BOIRE

ATTACH YOUR WINE LABEL HERE

BOIRE

PURCHASED AT: _____

PRICE: _____ DATE: _____

SHARED WITH: _____

_____ DATE: _____

PLACE: _____

MENU: _____

PERSONAL RATING: _____

COLOR: _____ BOUQUET: _____

TASTE: _____

NAME OF WINE: _____

VINTAGE YEAR: _____

VINTNER: _____

REGION: _____

QUI A LE CHAPEAU
SUR L'OREILLE.

ATTACH YOUR WINE LABEL HERE

QUI A LE CHAPEAU
SUR L'OREILLE.

PURCHASED AT: _____

PRICE: _____ DATE: _____

SHARED WITH: _____

_____ DATE: _____

PLACE: _____

MENU: _____

PERSONAL RATING: _____

COLOR: _____ BOUQUET: _____

TASTE: _____

NAME OF WINE: _____

VINTAGE YEAR: _____

VINTNER: _____

REGION: _____

ATTACH YOUR WINE LABEL HERE

PURCHASED AT: _____

PRICE: _____ DATE: _____

SHARED WITH: _____

_____ DATE: _____

PLACE: _____

MENU: _____

PERSONAL RATING: _____

COLOR: _____ BOUQUET: _____

TASTE: _____

NAME OF WINE: _____

VINTAGE YEAR: _____

VINTNER: _____

REGION: _____

LE VIN
LE PLUS
FORT

CHASSE

LE PLUS DELICAT

ATTACH YOUR WINE LABEL HERE

LE VIN
LE PLUS
FORT
CHASSE

LE PLUS dELICAT

PURCHASED AT: _____

PRICE: _____ DATE: _____

SHARED WITH: _____

_____ DATE: _____

PLACE: _____

MENU: _____

PERSONAL RATING: _____

COLOR: _____ BOUQUET: _____

TASTE: _____

NAME OF WINE: _____

VINTAGE YEAR: _____

VINTNER: _____

REGION: _____

Le poisson appelle Le rin blanc

ATTACH YOUR WINE LABEL HERE

Le poisson appelle Le vin blanc

PURCHASED AT: _____

PRICE: _____ DATE: _____

SHARED WITH: _____

_____ DATE: _____

PLACE: _____

MENU: _____

PERSONAL RATING: _____

COLOR: _____ BOUQUET: _____

TASTE: _____

NAME OF WINE: _____

VINTAGE YEAR: _____

VINTNER: _____

REGION: _____

ATTACH YOUR WINE LABEL HERE

PURCHASED AT: _____

PRICE: _____ DATE: _____

SHARED WITH: _____

_____ DATE: _____

PLACE: _____

MENU: _____

PERSONAL RATING: _____

COLOR: _____ BOUQUET: _____

TASTE: _____

NAME OF WINE: _____

VINTAGE YEAR: _____

VINTNER: _____

REGION: _____

ATTACH YOUR WINE LABEL HERE

PURCHASED AT: _____

PRICE: _____ DATE: _____

SHARED WITH: _____

_____ DATE: _____

PLACE: _____

MENU: _____

PERSONAL RATING: _____

COLOR: _____ BOUQUET: _____

TASTE: _____

NAME OF WINE: _____

VINTAGE YEAR: _____

VINTNER: _____

REGION: _____

QUI A DU CORSAGE

ATTACH YOUR WINE LABEL HERE

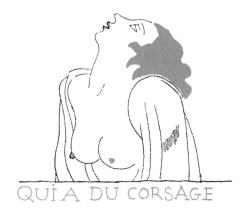

QUIA DU CORSAGE

PURCHASED AT: _____

PRICE: _____ DATE: _____

SHARED WITH: _____

_____ DATE: _____

PLACE: _____

MENU: _____

PERSONAL RATING: _____

COLOR: _____ BOUQUET: _____

TASTE: _____

NAME OF WINE: _____

VINTAGE YEAR: _____

VINTNER: _____

REGION: _____

ATTACH YOUR WINE LABEL HERE

PURCHASED AT: _____

PRICE: _____ DATE: _____

SHARED WITH: _____

_____ DATE: _____

PLACE: _____

MENU: _____

PERSONAL RATING: _____

COLOR: _____ BOUQUET: _____

TASTE: _____

NAME OF WINE: _____

VINTAGE YEAR: _____

VINTNER: _____

REGION: _____

ATTACH YOUR WINE LABEL HERE

La Cave

PURCHASED AT: _____

PRICE: _____ DATE: _____

SHARED WITH: _____

_____ DATE: _____

PLACE: _____

MENU: _____

PERSONAL RATING: _____

COLOR: _____ BOUQUET: _____

TASTE: _____

NAME OF WINE: _____

VINTAGE YEAR: _____

VINTNER: _____

REGION: _____

L'ÉLUE

ATTACH YOUR WINE LABEL HERE

L'ÉLUE

PURCHASED AT: _____

PRICE: _____ DATE: _____

SHARED WITH: _____

_____ DATE: _____

PLACE: _____

MENU: _____

PERSONAL RATING: _____

COLOR: _____ BOUQUET: _____

TASTE: _____

NAME OF WINE: _____

VINTAGE YEAR: _____

VINTNER: _____

REGION: _____

Le vin doit être vieux

ATTACH YOUR WINE LABEL HERE

Le vin doit être vieux

PURCHASED AT: _____

PRICE: _____ DATE: _____

SHARED WITH: _____

_____ DATE: _____

PLACE: _____

MENU: _____

PERSONAL RATING: _____

COLOR: _____ BOUQUET: _____

TASTE: _____

NAME OF WINE: _____

VINTAGE YEAR: _____

VINTNER: _____

REGION: _____

ATTACH YOUR WINE LABEL HERE

PURCHASED AT: _____

PRICE: _____ DATE: _____

SHARED WITH: _____

_____ DATE: _____

PLACE: _____

MENU: _____

PERSONAL RATING: _____

COLOR: _____ BOUQUET: _____

TASTE: _____

NAME OF WINE: _____

VINTAGE YEAR: _____

VINTNER: _____

REGION: _____

ATTACH YOUR WINE LABEL HERE

PURCHASED AT: _____

PRICE: _____ DATE: _____

SHARED WITH: _____

_____ DATE: _____

PLACE: _____

MENU: _____

PERSONAL RATING: _____

COLOR: _____ BOUQUET: _____

TASTE: _____

NAME OF WINE: _____

VINTAGE YEAR: _____

VINTNER: _____

REGION: _____

Cueillez Le Bouquet

ATTACH YOUR WINE LABEL HERE

Cueillez Le Bouquet

PURCHASED AT: _____

PRICE: _____ DATE: _____

SHARED WITH: _____

_____ DATE: _____

PLACE: _____

MENU: _____

PERSONAL RATING: _____

COLOR: _____ BOUQUET: _____

TASTE: _____

NAME OF WINE: _____

VINTAGE YEAR: _____

VINTNER: _____

REGION: _____

QUI A du CHIEN

ATTACH YOUR WINE LABEL HERE

Qui A du CHIEN

PURCHASED AT: _____

PRICE: _____ DATE: _____

SHARED WITH: _____

_____ DATE: _____

PLACE: _____

MENU: _____

PERSONAL RATING: _____

COLOR: _____ BOUQUET: _____

TASTE: _____

NAME OF WINE: _____

VINTAGE YEAR: _____

VINTNER: _____

REGION: _____

ATTACH YOUR WINE LABEL HERE

amadouez

Le

Petit Génie

PURCHASED AT: _____

PRICE: _____ DATE: _____

SHARED WITH: _____

_____ DATE: _____

PLACE: _____

MENU: _____

PERSONAL RATING: _____

COLOR: _____ BOUQUET: _____

TASTE: _____

NAME OF WINE: _____

VINTAGE YEAR: _____

VINTNER: _____

REGION: _____

La temperatura

ATTACH YOUR WINE LABEL HERE

PURCHASED AT: _____

PRICE: _____ DATE: _____

SHARED WITH: _____

_____ DATE: _____

PLACE: _____

MENU: _____

PERSONAL RATING: _____

COLOR: _____ BOUQUET: _____

TASTE: _____

NAME OF WINE: _____

VINTAGE YEAR: _____

VINTNER: _____

REGION: _____

ATTACH YOUR WINE LABEL HERE

POURQUOI !

PURCHASED AT: _____

PRICE: _____ DATE: _____

SHARED WITH: _____

_____ DATE: _____

PLACE: _____

MENU: _____

PERSONAL RATING: _____

COLOR: _____ BOUQUET: _____

TASTE: _____

NAME OF WINE: _____

VINTAGE YEAR: _____

VINTNER: _____

REGION: _____

Monseigneur le vin

ATTACH YOUR WINE LABEL HERE

Monseigneur le Vin

PURCHASED AT: _____

PRICE: _____ DATE: _____

SHARED WITH: _____

_____ DATE: _____

PLACE: _____

MENU: _____

PERSONAL RATING: _____

COLOR: _____ BOUQUET: _____

TASTE: _____

NAME OF WINE: _____

VINTAGE YEAR: _____

VINTNER: _____

REGION: _____

ATTACH YOUR WINE LABEL HERE

PURCHASED AT: _____

PRICE: _____ DATE: _____

SHARED WITH: _____

_____ DATE: _____

PLACE: _____

MENU: _____

PERSONAL RATING: _____

COLOR: _____ BOUQUET: _____

TASTE: _____

NAME OF WINE: _____

VINTAGE YEAR: _____

VINTNER: _____

REGION: _____

BOIRE

ATTACH YOUR WINE LABEL HERE

BOIRE

PURCHASED AT: _____

PRICE: _____ DATE: _____

SHARED WITH: _____

_____ DATE: _____

PLACE: _____

MENU: _____

PERSONAL RATING: _____

COLOR: _____ BOUQUET: _____

TASTE: _____

NAME OF WINE: _____

VINTAGE YEAR: _____

VINTNER: _____

REGION: _____

QUI A LE CHAPEAU
SUR L'OREILLE.

ATTACH YOUR WINE LABEL HERE

QUI A LE CHAPEAU
SUR L'OREILLE.

PURCHASED AT: _____

PRICE: _____ DATE: _____

SHARED WITH: _____

_____ DATE: _____

PLACE: _____

MENU: _____

PERSONAL RATING: _____

COLOR: _____ BOUQUET: _____

TASTE: _____

NAME OF WINE: _____

VINTAGE YEAR: _____

VINTNER: _____

REGION: _____

ATTACH YOUR WINE LABEL HERE

PURCHASED AT: _____

PRICE: _____ DATE: _____

SHARED WITH: _____

_____ DATE: _____

PLACE: _____

MENU: _____

PERSONAL RATING: _____

COLOR: _____ BOUQUET: _____

TASTE: _____

NAME OF WINE: _____

VINTAGE YEAR: _____

VINTNER: _____

REGION: _____

LE VIN
LE PLUS
FORT
CHASSE

LE PLUS DELICAT

ATTACH YOUR WINE LABEL HERE

LE VIN LE PLUS FORT CHASSE

LE PLUS DELICAT

PURCHASED AT: _____

PRICE: _____ DATE: _____

SHARED WITH: _____

_____ DATE: _____

PLACE: _____

MENU: _____

PERSONAL RATING: _____

COLOR: _____ BOUQUET: _____

TASTE: _____

NAME OF WINE: _____

VINTAGE YEAR: _____

VINTNER: _____

REGION: _____

Le poisson appelle Le vin blanc

ATTACH YOUR WINE LABEL HERE

Le poisson appelle Le vin blanc

PURCHASED AT: _____

PRICE: _____ DATE: _____

SHARED WITH: _____

_____ DATE: _____

PLACE: _____

MENU: _____

PERSONAL RATING: _____

COLOR: _____ BOUQUET: _____

TASTE: _____

NAME OF WINE: _____

VINTAGE YEAR: _____

VINTNER: _____

REGION: _____

ATTACH YOUR WINE LABEL HERE

PURCHASED AT: _____

PRICE: _____ DATE: _____

SHARED WITH: _____

_____ DATE: _____

PLACE: _____

MENU: _____

PERSONAL RATING: _____

COLOR: _____ BOUQUET: _____

TASTE: _____